Original title:
Laughing in the Lichen

Copyright © 2025 Creative Arts Management OÜ
All rights reserved.

Author: Mariana Leclair
ISBN HARDBACK: 978-1-80567-443-6
ISBN PAPERBACK: 978-1-80567-742-0

Nature's Delightful Echo

In the woods, the mushrooms play,
Whispers tickle leaves on sway.
Squirrel dons a mask of cheer,
Chasing shadows, drawing near.

Frogs croak jokes by the stream-side,
Ripples carry laughter wide.
Sunbeams through the branches peep,
While the turtles laugh and leap.

Comedies of the Canopy

A parrot cracks a silly pun,
As acorns fall, oh what fun!
Branches sway with playful glee,
In this towering jubilee.

The raccoons start a merry dance,
While fireflies join in a trance.
Leaves rustle with tickling tone,
Echoes of joy, all their own.

Revelry in the Understory

Beneath the ferns, a party brews,
With little ants in tiny shoes.
Beetles tap a rhythm sweet,
As the snails shuffle on their feet.

The shadows chuckle, teasing light,
A playful game in fading sight.
Dancing twigs and roots entwine,
In this secret, riotous shrine.

The Jolly Dance of the Forest Floor

Mossy carpets gently sway,
As critters join the wild ballet.
A wiggly worm takes center stage,
While a hedgehog turns the page.

Laughter echoes off the bark,
As shadows spark a tiny arc.
In the twilight, joy is found,
Where the natural hilarity abounds.

Smiles Through the Shrubbery

In the bushes, squirrels chat,
Bouncing here, there, and flat.
A thistle tickles a funny bone,
While petals giggle, all alone.

A bird in a hat struts with glee,
Chasing shadows, as fast as can be.
Caterpillars dance, what a sight,
Under the moon's silver light.

Amusing Antics of the Earth

Worms wear ties while spinning around,
Grasshoppers leap, they hardly touch ground.
A turtle's slow, yet quirky pace,
Leads to laughter in this wild place.

Dandelions puff like fluffy clouds,
Tickling all, drawing cheerful crowds.
Giggles float on warm summer air,
Earth's little jesters, beyond compare.

Teasing Tides of Tall Grasses

Waves of green dance in the breeze,
Whispers of mischief, if you please.
A ladybug wears polka-dot flair,
Hopping here and there without a care.

The wind joins in, with a playful hum,
Tickling tendrils, so carefree and dumb.
Bouncing buds in a joyful spree,
Nature's laughter, wild and free.

Cheer Beneath the Twisted Roots

Underneath where the gnarled trunks sway,
Critters gather for games in the fray.
A fox in a bowtie, so debonair,
Cracks a joke for the grinning hare.

A hedgehog rolls with a chuckling tune,
As fireflies wink at the giggling moon.
Deep in the soil, joy's infectious spread,
With roots that chuckle and stories unsaid.

Jovial Whirls of the Wind

The breeze dances lightly, full of glee,
Tickling the trees, oh so carefree.
Swaying the branches, a playful jest,
Nature giggles softly, feeling blessed.

In the meadow, a tumbleweed spins,
Bumping the daisies, where fun begins.
With every gust, a new story told,
As flowers join in, a sight to behold.

The clouds overhead, like fluff on a whip,
Drift by with a chuckle, a joyful trip.
They color the sky in a humorous sweep,
Also painting the dreams that we keep.

So let's spin and whirl, oh what a sight!
With giggles and wiggles, from morning to night.
For in this wild world, so merry and free,
The winds always whisper, just wait and see.

The Cackle of the Canopy

Amid the green leaves, a chorus will soar,
Branches giggle like never before.
A squirrel darts by, in rhymes, it dives,
As the shadows beneath begin to thrive.

The sun peeks through with a cheeky grin,
Casting its rays, where the fun will begin.
The birds sing a tune, a playful refrain,
While the forest erupts, in laughter and rain.

Fungi pop out, with colors so bright,
Mushrooms wearing hats, what a funny sight!
They wink and they nod, like friends in a crowd,
Spreading their joy, becoming quite loud.

Through canopies lush, with giggles that sway,
Every twig, every leaf, has a role in the play.
So let the trees cackle, and nature delight,
In this whimsical world, where joy takes flight.

Frolicsome Finds in Foliage

In the midst of leaves, a dance unfolds,
Silly shadows stretch, as mischief molds.
Beneath the fronds, a giggle hides,
With whispers of joy, where laughter bides.

Tiny critters scurry, a merry spree,
They tumble and roll, oh, wild jubilee!
Among the ferns, they plot and scheme,
Life's quirky rhythm is their lively dream.

Bliss in the Breezes of Briars

A breeze runs by, with a tickle and tease,
Swaying the branches with playful ease.
Whispers of cheer swirl in the air,
Briars entwine, with secrets to share.

The thorns wear smiles, as buds burst bright,
Colorful blooms dance, a joyful sight.
With every rustle, the laughter grows,
Carried on wind, where merriment flows.

Ecstatic Echoes of Earth

From under the soil, a chuckle erupts,
Earthworms wriggle, secrets they disrupt.
Roots intertwine with comedic flair,
The ground reverberates with joy in the air.

Tumbling stones hum with a rhythmic tune,
Under the stars, beneath the moon.
Each echoing giggle, a secret unsealed,
In the heart of the earth, all joy revealed.

Spirit of the Spiraling Vines

Around and around, the antics unfold,
Vines twist and turn, a story retold.
With hues of green, they swirl and sway,
Inviting all hearts to join in their play.

The spirit of fun in the tangled leaves,
Crafting sweet moments, as no one believes.
In every curl, a tale to embrace,
Nature's own laughter, a wild, warm space.

The Humor of Hidden Fungi

In the shadows they conspire,
Mushrooms with a wink,
Whisper secrets of the wood,
Nature's jesters, don't you think?

Caps that hold a smile bright,
Stems that sway with glee,
A tickle on the forest floor,
Where giggles sprout with glee.

Beneath the thick old boughs,
They gather for the jest,
Fungi frolic, spores take flight,
Their humor never rests.

With every step we take,
They giggle and they play,
A dance of whispers and of laughs,
In their own fungus way.

Delight Beneath the Ferns

Beneath the fronds, a party brews,
Tiny critters in a row,
Dancing in the morning dew,
To a tune we cannot know.

The ferns sway lightly in the breeze,
Tickling toes of passing feet,
While laughter hides in rustling leaves,
Nature's humor, pure and sweet.

A chorus sung by tiny things,
Echoes through the leafy dome,
Each chuckle springs from gentle springs,
This forest is their home.

With every shade and twist of green,
A punchline waits just out of sight,
Beneath the ferns, what fun is seen,
Where joy and nature unite.

To Be Light as a Spore

Floating through the air so free,
A spore dances, oh so spry,
Up to mischief, off it flees,
A giggle in the wind's soft sigh.

To be light as a spore, you see,
Brings a grin to every face,
Twirling whimsically, carefree,
In this wondrous, airy space.

A few more join the playful flight,
Jesting with the sun above,
In a world of pure delight,
Spore and laughter, hand in glove.

Each glimmering moment shared,
Turns the mundane into light,
As every tiny spore declared,
They'll spread joy, oh what a sight!

Chortles Amongst the Algae

In the depths where colors blend,
Algae swirl and stretch with cheer,
Their giggles bubble, never end,
Creating waves of joy, we hear.

Green and blue in playful binds,
Swaying gently, laugh and sway,
Dancing rhythm in the winds,
As sunlight smiles upon their play.

A shimmer here, a chuckle there,
They tickle toes of those who pass,
Nature's jesters without care,
Creating joy like gleaming glass.

So when you stroll beside the stream,
Listen close for their delight,
For among the algae's vibrant gleam,
Laughter greets you—what a sight!

Mischief Among the Mycelium

Tiny tricks in shadowed halls,
Fungi giggle as nature calls.
With every step, a soft surprise,
Beneath the ground, the laughter lies.

A rabbit hops with bated breath,
While roots conspire, they plot his death.
Yet in this jest, a dance unfolds,
As nature's whimsy laughs and scolds.

Whispers float on winds so light,
Mushrooms share a giggly fright.
Underneath the forest's cloak,
There's humor in the fungi joke.

Through the damp, the echoes prance,
Each spore a message, a silly dance.
The woodland knows this playful scheme,
In every patch, a dreamer's dream.

Chuckles in the Dappled Light

Sunlight spills through leafy beams,
As shadows play and nature schemes.
The leaves are tickled by the breeze,
Creating laughter in the trees.

A squirrel stumbles, then he grins,
In this moment, folly wins.
With acorns tossed in playful arcs,
His antics spark the woodland larks.

Dappled patches on the ground,
Whispers of giggles all around.
Each creature plays their comical role,
Nature's skit, a grand console.

Amidst the brush, a chorus sings,
What joy each little moment brings.
And in the brightness, all take flight,
Celebrating humor, pure delight.

Serene Smirks of Nature

In the morning, a gentle smile,
Nature revels without guile.
Rippling streams hum soft notes,
While rocks and pebbles share their quotes.

A turtle grins with patient grace,
Slow and steady wins the race.
But in the grass, a secret jest,
The rabbits giggle, never rest.

The sunbeams wink on ferny fronds,
Frogs croak out in playful bonds.
Under this leafy, twinkling roof,
Each joyous sigh is nature's hoof.

With every breeze that passes by,
The flowers dance and seem to sigh.
In this realm of playful cheer,
The smirks of nature draw us near.

Frolics in the Forest Floor

On the forest floor, the fun begins,
With mushrooms mischievous like cheeky twins.
Rabbits race through paths so wide,
While nature laughs, her joy a tide.

With every leap, a silly sound,
As creatures lose themselves, unbound.
Ants march strict, but there's delight,
In tiny dances, day and night.

Beneath the brush, the whispers grow,
A playhouse perfect; do they know?
Each rustling leaf, a giggly tease,
Invites the woodland folk to seize.

In this playful, vibrant maze,
Life's sweet folly earns our praise.
Nature hosts this grand affair,
With laughter woven in the air.

The Sway of a Happy Spore

In a tiny world where mushrooms sway,
A spore skips joyfully, bright as day.
With a giggle here and a wiggle there,
It twirls around without a care.

Bouncing off roots and jumping on stones,
Mossy friends greet with cheerful tones.
Each little bounce brings a peal of delight,
Underneath the warm sunlight.

A toadstool chuckles as it grows tall,
Its cap tipping just to share with all.
The dance of life is playful and sweet,
In this enchanting, tiny retreat.

So come and join in this merry affair,
With spores above in the crisp, fresh air.
Nature's giggle fills every nook,
In the heart of the forest, take a look.

Joyful Shadows in the Wood

In dappled light where shadows prance,
Fungi join in a merry dance.
Elfin whispers swirl around,
With laughter hidden in the ground.

A squirrel itches up a tree,
Tickled by branches, oh so free!
The wind hums a tune that's funky,
As light-footed critters get all spunky.

Every rustle brings a silly grin,
Bright little eyes ready for spin.
Mushrooms giggle under leafy hats,
Playing games with the cheeky bats.

So let your spirit take a flight,
Join this party, pure delight!
In the woods where shadows glide,
Joy and mischief so collide.

Grins in Glistening Dew

Morning breaks with a sparkling cheer,
Dewdrops shimmer, giggling near.
Each tiny orb holds a secret laugh,
Nature's jewels on a grassy staff.

Ants parade in their shiny suits,
Dancing 'round the tiny roots.
A playful breeze gives them a spin,
A waltz in the warmth, let the fun begin!

Ferns unfurl like ticklish hands,
Waving at the curious bands.
With a glee that seems to wind,
In the morning light, joy you'll find.

In every droplet, the laughter swells,
A symphony of sweet, tiny bells.
So wander softly and take a cue,
From the grins in glistening dew.

The Playful Dance of Lichens

On rocky edges where colors blend,
Lichens chuckle, round every bend.
With patches bright, they skip and spin,
Whispering secrets they cheekily grin.

A patch of green lets out a cheer,
As the sunlight shines, it's crystal clear.
Tiny creatures peek and play,
In the vibrant hues, they come out to sway.

Mingling in silence, they rise and fall,
Creating laughter that echoes through all.
With every storm that passes by,
They dance like jesters beneath the sky.

So wander close and take a glance,
At the playful dance, give it a chance!
In nature's gallery, joy resides,
Where lichens bloom and laughter abides.

Whispers of the Woodland

In the glade where shadows play,
Squirrels chatter, come what may,
Frogs wear tiny, crooked grins,
Sending ripples, laughter spins.

Wiggly worms in a merry race,
Wobble with a wiggly grace,
The trees chuckle, leaves a-dance,
Nature's jesters, take a chance!

Breezes blow with chuckles sweet,
While rabbits hop on little feet,
Mushrooms giggle, slightly shy,
Underneath the open sky.

As twilight paints the forest gold,
Little critters brave and bold,
Join in jest, a merry choir,
In the wood, the fun won't tire.

Giggling Among the Green

In the fields where daisies dance,
Bumblebees with goofy prance,
They zip and zoom, oh what a sight,
Creating chaos, pure delight!

Dewdrops glisten, glimmer bright,
A chorus sings, both day and night,
Gentle winds, they sway and tease,
Whispering secrets through the leaves.

Frolicking fawns, all in a line,
Playful struggles, never benign,
Underneath the oaks they leap,
Spreading joy in laughter deep.

And when the stars begin to blink,
The fireflies join in, don't you think?
With twinkling lights that wink and sway,
In nature's jest, they find their play.

Joy in the Mossy Shadows

In the coolness of the shade,
Mossy banks where children played,
The critters peek, with giggles loud,
Jestful whispers, nature's crowd.

Bunnies hop, their ears a-flop,
Tickled feet that never stop,
Spinny snails in races slow,
On slippery paths, they steal the show!

Underneath the elder trees,
Chirping birds are sure to tease,
A wobbly fox, eyes full of fun,
Chasing his tail, he's on the run!

With laughter echoing soft and sweet,
In the twilight, life's a treat,
From shadows deep, the joy does bloom,
In every nook, there's fun to loom.

Delights of the Underbrush

In the thicket, treasures roam,
Tiny critters make a home,
Gaudy beetles, dressed to play,
Stir up giggles every day.

Ladybugs with polka dots,
Dance on mossy, comfy spots,
Picky snails with sticky trails,
Share their laughs in tiny gales.

Shadows lengthen, stories spun,
A wild cat joins in the fun,
Eyes a-twinkle, tails that sway,
Nature's mischief on display!

As moonbeams touch the forest floor,
The merry sounds of joy encore,
In underbrush, where secrets lie,
Laughter echoes through the sky.

Grins Beneath the Bark

In shadows where the creatures peek,
The woodlands chuckle, soft and sleek.
A squirrel spins a tale so grand,
While mushrooms dance, hand in hand.

The tree trunks twist with glee, it seems,
Nature's jesters weave their dreams.
A raccoon pranks with playful tricks,
While crickets play their rhythmic licks.

Around the roots, the laughter swirls,
As tiny, timid toads do twirls.
With every rustle, giggles burst,
In hidden nooks where fun is first.

So join the fun beneath the shade,
Where every critter's laugh won't fade.
For in this place, the humor grows,
A joyful joke where no one knows.

Sprightly Secrets of the Soil

The earth has whispers, sly and light,
Where bugs play games amidst the night.
With giggles soft as mossy beds,
They share their tales, and none misreads.

A worm does waltz, a beetle prance,
In hidden realms, they take their chance.
They wiggle, jiggle, twist and turn,
In rich, dark realms where secrets churn.

A root unveils a minty tease,
While ants conspire on gentle breeze.
With every tumble in the dirt,
They spread their joy; no one gets hurt.

In soil so deep, where laughter's rife,
A merry dance springs forth from life.
These sprightly secrets, earthy, bold,
In nature's arms, their joy unfolds.

Amusement in the Ferns

In leafy realms where ferns sway bright,
The whispers bubble up with delight.
A frond does sway, a ticklish tease,
While dew drops giggle on their knees.

With ladybugs in dotted gowns,
They twirl about, in joyous rounds.
The shadows laugh and dance around,
As froggy tunes echo profound.

Amongst the greens, the jesters play,
A dance of life, a bright display.
With every rustle, chuckles bloom,
In crowded nooks, joy finds room.

So frolic here, 'neath leafy scenes,
Where laughter thrives in gentle greens.
With every step, a quip awaits,
In fern-filled havens, fun creates.

Jovial Mists of the Thicket

Through misty paths where shadows tease,
The thicket laughs upon the breeze.
With whispered winds, the stories sail,
A playful shout, a fleeting trail.

A fox trots by with a knowing grin,
While playful shadows draw you in.
Amongst the roots, the magic's near,
As echoes of joy light up the sphere.

In twilight's hush, the tales arise,
Of merry pranks in moonlit skies.
The laughter weaves through branches tight,
In tangled knots of pure delight.

So venture forth where spirits roam,
In jovial mists, you'll find a home.
With every giggle, make your mark,
In wondrous woods, where joy won't hark.

Uproar in the Underbrush

A squirrel in a dance, what a sight,
Chasing shadows, filled with delight.
A rabbit trips, with a twisty spin,
Pine cones laughing, let the fun begin!

Frogs leap high, like a springy spring,
Wobbling like they own the king.
Butterflies giggle, in colorful swirls,
Tickling the toes of the dancing girls.

Bumblebees buzzing, tickle their noses,
While clovers whisper, oh how it dozes.
A fox in a hat, what a charming spree,
Tiptoeing softly, as sly as can be!

Amid the chaos, a tune arises,
Leaves swaying gently, nature's prizes.
In the underbrush, silliness reigns,
With every giggle, forget your pains!

Mirthful Moments in the Meadow

In the meadow, giggles soar high,
Dandelion seeds float on by.
A cow with a moo that tickles the air,
Raises a chuckle, oh what a flair!

Grasshoppers hop to a bouncy beat,
While daisies cheer on with warmth and sweet.
A sunbeam slips through, a mischievous tease,
Painting smiles on the clouds with ease.

Look at the field, where shadows blend,
Every step brings a merry trend.
A wind that whispers funny tales,
Of bunnies in tuxedos, and funny gales.

When day dreams, and laughter collide,
Joy wraps us in a giggly glide.
In this meadow, hearts entwine,
With every chuckle, all's divine!

Glee Among the Grey

In the mist, where shadows play,
A crow in a bowtie steals the day.
With a caw so sharp, he takes a bow,
Blowing kisses, oh, take a wow!

Fungi sprout with funny hats,
Making grins that disarm all spats.
A hedgehog rolls in a playful spree,
Wobbling past, so joyfully free.

Clouds peek through with a cheeky grin,
Helping the sun throw a spontaneous spin.
A raindrop tickles the nose of a snail,
Leads him to ponder, should I set sail?

Gryphons in rocks form giggly traits,
While the brook babbles about the great mates.
In the grey, a resonating cheer,
Life dances along, never in fear!

Playful Patches of Green

In patches so bright, the giggles abound,
With daisies buggy dancing all around.
A ladybug winks with a funny jest,
Creeping on curls, it's nature's quest!

With each swish, the grasses foxtrot,
A chubby caterpillar gives it all a shot.
Bumblebees gather for a prancing show,
As a carrot in the ground says, "Don't be slow!"

Peeking from bushes, a gopher with glee,
Spinning a yarn as charming as can be.
While sunflowers nod, in gentle embrace,
Making merry in this open space.

In playful patches, joy intertwines,
With every laughter, the heart aligns.
So stroll through this green, where smiles are free,
Join in the jest, come dance with me!

Whimsical Whispers of the Wild

In the woods where shadows play,
Mushrooms dance in bright array.
Squirrels giggle, tails held high,
As butterflies float, oh so spry.

Crickets chirp a silly tune,
While the flowers sway, a joyful boon.
Each leaf whispers secrets, so light,
In the chorus of day and night.

Bubbles of laughter tickle the air,
A playful breeze brings joyful flair.
Branches sway with hapless trees,
Nature smiles with such sweet ease.

And when the sun dips low and warm,
Fungi giggle through a gentle storm.
The wild blooms with tales so bright,
In every nook, pure delight.

Harmony in the Hidden Hinterlands.

In the glade where stories grow,
Giggling streams in the sun's soft glow.
Hiding places call with glee,
To playful sprites, wild and free.

Leaves chatter with a rustling sound,
Peculiar antics, joy unbound.
The wind carries chuckles around,
As rabbits hop without a sound.

Twisted branches wriggle and bend,
With fairy giggles that never end.
Mossy carpets where we all play,
Bring smiles to brighten the day.

In secret nooks, where mischief brews,
Nature's laughter in vibrant hues.
Harmony sings in every rustle,
A hidden world in playful tussle.

Whispers of Mossy Joy

Beneath the trees where shadows sprout,
A ticklish breeze wanders about.
Mossy beds and spongy ground,
Echo joyful sounds all around.

Toadstools tell of silly dreams,
While sunshine dances in warm beams.
Ants parade with tiny glee,
Creating stories as they flee.

The fern fronds wave with a soft cheer,
Tickling toes as they draw near.
Nature's humor, light and sly,
Makes even the tallest oak sigh.

With every step, laughter grows,
Among the ferns and the lilac bows.
Whispers twinkling beneath the sky,
In this secret realm of sprightly high.

Under the Canopy of Giggles

Branches sway like children play,
Laughing leaves on a sunny day.
Beneath the boughs, the world is bright,
Giggling sprites dance with delight.

Clouds above parade and tease,
While flowers twist with playful ease.
The grass winks, a mischievous sight,
Coaxed by sunbeams, warm and light.

A curious squirrel, so spry and slick,
Plays peek-a-boo with a little flick.
The mushrooms grin, so round and bold,
Whispering secrets, tales untold.

As dusk descends, the sprites take flight,
Spreading laughter throughout the night.
Under the stars, they spin and swirl,
In this symphony, joy unfurl.

Smiles Among the Soil

Tiny critters dance and play,
Giggling while they dig away.
With little shovels made of leaves,
They plant the jokes that nature weaves.

Mushrooms wear their caps so high,
They perch like clowns beneath the sky.
Roots tangle in a silly race,
While whispers tickle every place.

Worms tell tales of wormy fun,
Underneath the glowing sun.
Each twist and turn a playful tease,
Among the flora, hearts at ease.

What a sight, this joyful ground,
Where hidden giggles can be found.
Embrace the earth, its lively call,
For smiles abound, let laughter sprawl.

Whimsy Among Wet Wonders

Raindrops bounce like tiny friends,
In puddles where the laughter blends.
Splashes echo, sparking glee,
As frogs hop out for a spree.

The shy snails leave their trails of fun,
Each spiral's like a race begun.
They slide with grace, quite unaware,
That laughter's waiting everywhere.

Leaves drape down with a twinkle bright,
Crafting shadows, dancing light.
Nature jesting in each bend,
Inviting all to join and lend.

Amidst the drizzle, joy's alive,
With every splash, the spirits thrive.
Whimsy blooms beneath the gray,
In every drop, a joke at play.

Cheer in the Creeping Clovers

Cloaked in green, the clovers grin,
With winks that whisper where to begin.
A four-leaf gem, a playful quest,
Hiding jokes that never rest.

Bees buzz by with cheeky tunes,
Sipping nectar 'neath the moons.
Each buzz a chuckle, light and bright,
Filling the meadow, pure delight.

Little ants make rows, parade,
With every stride, a joke is laid.
They march in step, a comic crew,
Planning mischief, just for you.

Every patch, a stage for cheer,
Where nature's laughter comes so near.
With every step through clover's maze,
The heart finds joy in sunny days.

Banter of the Bark

The trees exchange their wildest tales,
As squirrels listen, twitching tails.
Branches twist in riotous glee,
Sharing secrets of the spree.

Knots in bark hide jokes untold,
Wisdom shared from young and old.
Whispers swirl in leafy cover,
With each rustle, a new discover.

A chipmunk chimes in, chipper and clear,
With tales of harvest, have you heard?
The laughter echoes through the wood,
As nature's pranks are understood.

Underneath the old oak's shade,
The banter blooms, and hearts cascade.
Laughter dances in the breeze,
With every joke, the forest frees.

Blissful Echoes of Woodland

In the shade where shadows dance,
Mushrooms wear their silly hats.
Squirrels chat in ribald trance,
While frogs croak funny spats.

The flowers giggle in the breeze,
As bumblebees spin round and round.
A chorus sung amidst the trees,
Life's humor in nature found.

Dancing leaves in vibrant glee,
Lift the hearts of passersby.
The brook joins in, a melody,
As fish leap up to try to fly.

With every snicker, rustle, sigh,
The woodland weaves its joyful song.
Underneath the blushing sky,
Where cheerful spirits all belong.

The Glee Beneath the Layers

Mossy carpets soaked in cheer,
Hide the giggles of the ground.
Every step brings forth a cheer,
As laughter in the soil is found.

Caterpillars with wiggly flair,
Wobble in a festive line.
While ants march on, without a care,
Piling crumbs like little twine.

Raccoons don their masks at night,
Planning pranks beneath the stars.
Their antics spark a pure delight,
As fireflies join in with sparklers.

Gloomy clouds can't hold us down,
With jests that never seem to end.
In laughter's trail, no time to frown,
For joy's the treasure we defend.

Enchanted Laughter Among Leaves

Up above, the branches sway,
Where whispers hide in shades of green.
The wind carries jokes at play,
In nature's air, a silly scene.

A playful breeze tickles the ferns,
While the old oak shakes with glee.
Each twist and turn, the laughter churns,
Echoing through the woods so free.

The raccoon giggles beneath the stars,
As owls hoot in a quirky beat.
While the world spins on, it's never far,
From joyous sounds soft and sweet.

Every rustle brings a grin,
Each fluttered leaf has tales to tell.
In this woodland, joy's our kin,
With laughter weaving every spell.

Silly Whispers of the Wild

Listen close, the wild things speak,
With hiccuped breaths and chuckling sounds.
A playful breeze, so warm and cheek,
Through trees it swirls and whirls around.

The bunnies leap and bounce with flair,
Sharing secrets as they dart.
Giggling softly, without a care,
As tiny creatures play their part.

In fields where dandelions sway,
A breeze tosses petals like confetti.
Each little puff, a hearty play,
Stirs joy that's light and ever ready.

At dawn, the sky wears a smile,
As sunbeams stretch and chase the dew.
In nature's grip, we rest awhile,
Where every giggle feels brand new.

Whimsy in the Wilderness

In the woods where shadows play,
Frogs wear hats and dance all day.
Trees wear smiles, branches sway,
Nature's jesters lead the way.

Squirrels chatter, tails on fire,
With their antics, they inspire.
Beneath the sun, all creatures cheer,
Laughter echoes, loud and clear.

Bunnies hop with silly grace,
Chasing threads in a wild race.
Butterflies take flight and dive,
In this place, all things come alive.

So join the fun, let spirits soar,
In the wild, there's always more.
Every rustle holds a joke,
In this realm where laughter's woke.

Euphoria on the Bark

On textured trunks, the stories spin,
Beetles dance, they always win.
Mossy hats and twinkling eyes,
Nature's jesters in disguise.

Fluffy clouds in the bright blue sky,
Play tag with sunlight, oh so spry.
Wink and chuckle, breezes tease,
Whispers laughing through the leaves.

Nuts and acorns roll around,
Making chords of playful sound.
A tree frog croaks a heartfelt song,
In this world where all belong.

Join the revelry, take a seat,
In this forest, joy's complete.
With every step, a giggle springs,
In the heart of nature's whims.

The Humor of Nature's Layers

Under rocks where secrets hide,
Worms wear outfits, oh, so wide!
Fungi giggle, colors bright,
Their nature's charm brings pure delight.

In the meadow, daisies grin,
Their petals twirl, and tumble in.
Ants march by with tiny pride,
In their world, there's nowhere to hide.

Each layer holds a tale to tell,
Of unexpected laughs that swell.
In the breeze, a funny tune,
Nature's laughter, afternoon.

So lift your gaze and join the fun,
In this realm where all is spun.
Every creature plays a part,
In this comedy that warms the heart.

Sunshine's Tickling Touch

Sunshine dances on the leaves,
Working wonders, nature weaves.
Fluttering wings, a ticklish tease,
With every ray, the world agrees.

Dew drops giggle on the grass,
Winking as the shadows pass.
Crickets chirp their silly rhymes,
In a symphony of chimes.

Bees in bloom, they buzz about,
Chasing pollen, roundabout.
With every buzz, a joke they share,
Creating laughter in the air.

So step outside, let joy ignite,
Beneath the sun's warm, cheerful light.
In this bright and lively clutch,
Feel the warmth of sunshine's touch.

Joyfilling Journeys of From Root to Tree

Tiny roots wiggle with glee,
Poking through soil, as sprightly as can be.
Leaves whisper secrets, they giggle and sway,
Each branch a jester, come join the play!

Sunlight tickles the bark and the bud,
While shadows dance with a playful thud.
Squirrels share jokes in a chattery spree,
Nature's own laughter, wild and free!

Rain drops like marbles, on petals they land,
Creating a symphony, so whimsically grand.
The whispers of foliage, a chuckle so bold,
With stories of mischief, forever retold!

In the embrace of the breeze, we find delight,
As the shadows and sunlight twist day into night.
From root to the crown, let joy intertwine,
In this endless frolic, where thoughts brightly shine!

The Restless Revelers of the Moss

Moss gathers round for a lively chat,
Wobbling and bobbing, just like a hat.
With tiny green dancers held in a trance,
They sway to the rhythm of a mischievous dance.

In puddles they leap, with splashes so bold,
Each droplet a laughter, a story to be told.
The lichen-laced pranks echo through the day,
As nature provides a comical play!

With a tickle of dew, the giggles arise,
As critters join in, all colors and sizes.
The mossy brigade, with joy leading the way,
Turns the mundane into a whimsical play.

When twilight approaches, the stars come alive,
In the hush of the night, the revelers thrive.
Underneath the soft glow of the silvery moon,
They whisper their secrets, in a jovial tune!

Hilarity Among the Herbaceous

Herbs stand in clusters, a riotous scene,
With basil, thyme, and parsley, they preen.
Thyme tells a joke, as sage rolls her eyes,
While rosemary giggles, to nobody's surprise!

Amidst the tall stalks, there's laughter galore,
As petals are tossed and the wind starts to roar.
Dandelion wishes float high in the air,
While mint makes a quip, it's all quite a fare!

Under the sun's gaze, the comedy blooms,
As blossoms ignite, dispelling the glooms.
They chatter and banter, their leaves all aglow,
Creating a melody, sweet and playful flow.

In gardens of joy, the herbaceous unite,
With snickers and snorts, they delight in the night.
Their fragrance enchanting, can brighten a day,
With humor and heart, they shine in their way!

Scribbles of Smiles in the Soil

Beneath the earth, where the giggles reside,
Tiny critters dig in, with smiles that glide.
Worms twist and turn, with their squiggly flair,
Creating a riddle, hidden with care.

The roots pen stories of growth and of fun,
As beetles buzz round, enjoying the sun.
With every small tickle of soil's soft embrace,
The whispers of laughter bring joy to the place.

Caterpillars wiggle, with names on their lips,
As ants march in line, sharing comical quips.
Together they scribble a tale of pure cheer,
With rhymes made of dirt, to the heart they endear!

In this magical realm, where humor can bloom,
With each silly twist, there's plenty of room.
For smiles are the scribbles that life can bestow,
In the depths of the earth, the joy ever grows!

Radiance in the Rugged Roots

Beneath the boughs, a giggle grows,
Roots entwined in silly prose.
Mushrooms dance, a wobbly show,
Nature's jest is all aglow.

Squirrels chatter, cheeky and spry,
In their caps, they whisper, "Why?"
Upside down, the world seems bright,
Even shadows find delight.

A frog croaks jokes with comic flair,
Raining laughter on the air.
Ferns wave arms in wavy cheer,
Tickled leaves, they splinter near.

In rugged realms where sunbeams gleam,
Every creature lives the dream.
Roots and laughter intertwined,
A jolly echo, purely kind.

Elation in the Emerald Enclave

In emerald shades, giggles sprout,
Every twist, a jest without doubt.
Breezes tickle the playful ferns,
Whispers shared, as the laughter churns.

Crickets chirp in perfect rhyme,
Nature's band invites the thyme.
With every rustling leaf on high,
The trees join in, oh my, oh my!

Toads in slippers hop with glee,
Cheering on the bumblebee.
In this enclave, joy's the tune,
As daisies sway beneath the moon.

Such merriment in colors bright,
Emerald dances shine with light.
Every corner hums with cheer,
In this place where smiles appear.

Gleeful Groves

In the groves where mischief flows,
Laughter tumbles, tickles toes.
Branches wave with playful tricks,
While shadows play their little flicks.

Bunnies hop on rubbery feet,
Trying to chase their own heartbeat.
Sunbeams peek through leafy screens,
Giggling brightly, bursting scenes.

With hidden pranks and jokes so sly,
The owls wink as they pass by.
Blades of grass tickle the toes,
In this glade where joy just grows.

Each step brings a new charade,
In gleeful groves, no plans are made.
Laughter spills, it gathers round,
Where silly tales and smiles abound.

Revelry in the Rambunctious Reeds

The reeds are wild, a playful crew,
They sway and jig as if they knew.
Whispers run with every breeze,
Chasing giggles through the trees.

Frogs in hats, they leap and tease,
Crafting songs with swaying ease.
Each pluck of string brings roars of glee,
In this revelry, wild and free.

Waves of laughter bounce and play,
Sprinkling joy throughout the day.
Feathers flutter, high they soar,
Rambunctious crew, we ask for more!

Twilight glimmers, the fun won't end,
In reed-filled realms, where hearts ascend.
Every cackle, every cheer,
The world rejoices, full of mirth and cheer.

Fun Beneath the Balance of Branches

Beneath the trees where shadows play,
Squirrels dance in a quirky ballet.
Leaves swirl down, like giggling sprites,
Tickling the ground with their silly sights.

A chubby chipmunk lets out a cheer,
As acorns tumble, oh what a deer!
Branches bend low, as if to tease,
While the breeze whispers secrets with ease.

The owls hoot odd, with eyes so wide,
While mushrooms form a fun, spongy ride.
When winds blow softly, they swirl and spin,
In nature's circus, let the fun begin.

So come and frolic, join in the spree,
Under the branches, just you and me.
With every rustle, there's laughter anew,
In this whimsical world where joy breaks through.

Nectar of the Laughing Leaves

In gardens where the blossoms grin,
The nectar flows with a playful spin.
Bees buzz in tunes, oh what a sound,
As flowers share secrets, all around.

Petals unfurl with a giggly sway,
While ants march by in a jolly parade.
Sunlight sparkles on dew-kissed bows,
Tickling the nose, laughter flows.

A dandelion puffs with a puff,
Spreading its wishes, never too tough.
The world is painted with joy so bright,
In this sweet haven, from morning to night.

So come and taste this zestful cheer,
In fields where we laugh without any fear.
With every sip, the world feels light,
As nature's nectar makes hearts take flight.

The Gathered Grins of Growth

Amongst the sprouts where giggles bloom,
There's magic hiding in every room.
Tiny roots chuckle beneath the clay,
As they stretch and yawn, welcoming play.

The vines twist tightly, like a big hug,
While ladybugs waltz on a lovebug.
Sunflowers nod in a jolly tune,
While shadows sway in the warm afternoon.

Frogs croak melodies, offbeat but bright,
Chasing each other in a leafy flight.
Their silly jumps bring bursts of glee,
In this wild wonder, oh come and see!

So gather 'round for the show that's due,
With each little giggle, the grass feels new.
Nature's own laughter, a joyful decree,
In this garden party, just you and me.

Play in the Petal's Shade

Under petals soft, where shadows blend,
Creatures frolic, no need to pretend.
Butterflies flutter, a colorful race,
In the secret nooks, they find their space.

Grasshoppers leap, with a comical air,
Like acrobats flying without any care.
The daisies giggle, their heads held high,
As the clouds drift lazily in the blue sky.

In the foliage, secrets flicker and shine,
Where friends share stories, all intertwined.
Nature's trampoline bursts with delight,
As we play and frolic from morning to night.

So find your joy in this lush escapade,
With hearts wide open, let laughter cascade.
In every rustle, there's a moment to seize,
In the petal's embrace, we find our ease.

Joyful Journeys through the Juniper

Beneath the boughs, where shadows play,
A squirrel spins in a dizzy ballet.
The juniper whispers a secret tune,
While butterflies dance 'neath the bright afternoon.

Through winding paths where the rabbits race,
A jolly frog joins the frolicsome chase.
With giggles that echo in sun-drenched air,
Each twist and turn leads to cheerful repair.

The breeze, a jester, tickles the leaves,
While sunbeams wink through the light-hearted eaves.
Every step brings forth a chuckle or two,
In this merry maze of the green and the blue.

So come along, let's skip and twirl,
Through joyful journeys as giggles unfurl.
In every nook, let happiness reign,
As we wander, enchanted by laughter's sweet train.

The Merry Mirth of Moss

In the soft embrace of emerald spread,
Moss cradles dreams in its verdant bed.
The tiny critters hold a grand parade,
Spinning tales of joy that never will fade.

Amidst the stones, a chipmunk grins wide,
As plump little toads hop and slide.
Each gentle squish beneath our feet,
Is a playful jest that feels so sweet.

Chortles echo through the forest floor,
As woodland gnomes craft their mischief galore.
In every tuft where little ones hide,
Laughter bubbles like the softest tide.

So join the revel, let's lay on the green,
In the merry mirth where the unseen is seen.
With each breath taken, let happiness flow,
In the cozy moss where our spirits glow.

Laughter in the Leafy Labyrinth

In a maze of greens where shadows flicker,
Life has a laugh, and it's bound to stick here.
The leaves whisper secrets with a cheerful tease,
As silly squirrels scamper with utmost ease.

Twisted trails play tricks on the mind,
With giggles echoing, joy intertwined.
Each corner turned brings a new surprise,
As a grinning hedgehog rolls, oh what a guise!

Winding about, let's frolic and spin,
Through the leafy lanes where the fun begins.
With every soft chuckle, we'll map out the way,
In this jolly labyrinth where we wish to stay.

So gather your friends, let's dance through the day,
In the leafy playground where laughter holds sway.
With hearts intertwining, a moment sublime,
In the labyrinth's embrace, we'll frolic through time.

Serenade of the Subterranean

Beneath the earth, where the mushrooms gleam,
Frogs strike a chord in a jovial dream.
The beetles march forth in a rhythmic parade,
While the wise old worms chuckle, in shade.

In tunnels rich with aromas so bright,
Creatures conspire to bring pure delight.
With whispers and giggles, they plot and they scheme,
A subterranean world birthed from a dream.

The roots intertwine, sharing tales of the morn,
While fairies in hiding play harps of forlorn.
Each plucky note flutters on up through the soil,
Where the joy of the underground begins to uncoil.

So listen closely to the mirth that you find,
In the serenade crafted by nature so kind.
In the depths of the earth where whimsy takes flight,
Let laughter resound in the coolness of night.

Ecstasy of Earthy Edges

Beneath the soil, a giggle grows,
Mossy whispers from the toes.
Frogs wear crowns, and snails parade,
In nature's jest, unbothered shade.

Tiny fungi dance and twirl,
With cap and cloak, they spin and swirl.
The earth, alive with chuckles sweet,
In every corner, a playful treat.

Rocks wear smiles, so round and bright,
While shadows play hide-and-seek at night.
Each pebble cracks a silly rhyme,
A comedy of the verdant clime.

So tiptoe where the daisies wink,
And let the evening air make you think.
For in the depths of green delight,
Laughter bubbles, a pure delight.

Frolic in the Ferns

Ferns are twirling, bright and green,
A leafy jig, a joyful scene.
Breezes tickle as they prance,
Nature's jesters in a dance.

Squirrels giggle, tails held high,
Chasing shadows, oh, how they fly!
Each leap is met with cheerful cheer,
In the ferns, there's nothing to fear.

Crickets chirp a playful tune,
Underneath the watching moon.
Every rustle, a chuckle shared,
In this frolic, all are bared.

So join the fun, don't hesitate,
In the ferns, there's laughing fate.
With every step, let joy be found,
A merry world is all around.

Tickles of Treetop Tales

Up in the boughs, where the breezes play,
Woodpeckers joke throughout the day.
Branches bend with laughter loud,
Underneath the leafy crowd.

Chirping birds throw gags galore,
With each flutter, they soar and explore.
A raucous league of feathered friends,
In the trees, the fun never ends.

Squirrels chatter, tossing acorns,
Making mischief until the morn.
Each nut a treasure, a squirrel's jest,
Offering giggles, never a rest.

So climb the hills and touch the sky,
For nature's comedians never shy.
In every breeze, a secret pails,
Tickling hearts with treetop tales.

Jests of the Gnarled Roots

Roots curl and twist, like a jester's grin,
In the underbrush, where the fun begins.
Tangled tales and stories weave,
As the forest laughs, and we believe.

A badger scampers, stumbling near,
In the muddy patch, he finds the cheer.
Every slip amidst the leaves,
Brings forth giggles that the earth receives.

Beneath the bark, the whispers float,
While critters plot on a willow's note.
Each shadow moves with a secret fun,
Until the day succumbs to sun.

So wander low where the roots have depth,
Discover smiles in every step.
In gnarled humor, we find our play,
In nature's comedy, we stay all day.

Chuckles Beneath the Canopy

Under the leaves, a whispering joy,
Mushrooms giggle, each spore a toy.
Squirrels tease with a tail in the air,
Nature's jesters, without a care.

Rain drops dance on a ferny floor,
As the wind tells jokes to the trees galore.
Brightly colored bugs join the spree,
With winks and wiggles, so carefree.

Sunlight streams through a green-draped scene,
Casting laughter where all have been.
A rare blossom bursts, a sight so neat,
With petals like giggles that can't be beat.

Beneath the boughs, where shadows abound,
A chorus of chuckles is joyfully found.
In nature's arms, whimsy is spun,
Under the canopy, the fun's just begun.

Hilarity in Hidden Havens

In a thicket where secrets reside,
Beetles parade on a leafy ride.
Curled ferns act out a playful charade,
While the sun peeks in, unafraid.

Here in the nooks, the laughter aligns,
Frogs croak jokes in sweet, silly rhymes.
A rabbit hops, not making a sound,
With a wiggle so funny, he spins all around.

Moss-covered rocks, a comfy retreat,
Where the critters gather to play and meet.
Each sound is a laugh in the whispering shade,
In hidden havens, the game's not delayed.

The breeze carries giggles, so breezy and light,
As fireflies flicker, a glowing delight.
What joy it creates, this organic affair,
In corners secluded, where humor's laid bare.

Mirth Among the Microbes

Tiny taunts from the microbial crew,
Where unseen jesters concoct their brew.
With squishy laughter beneath our feet,
In the soil's embrace, the fun's bittersweet.

Bacteria dance in a wiggly race,
Spreading smiles in the dampest place.
With spores that giggle and wiggle with glee,
They turn mundane dirt into comedy.

Fungi feasting with a chuckle that spreads,
In the unseen world, where whimsy treads.
Every squirm and wiggle a jolly surprise,
In the realm of the small, where humor flies.

Amidst the microbes, the joy has its start,
With nature's own jests, tugging at our heart.
The smallest of beings can bring such delight,
In the tiniest worlds, they shine ever bright.

Grins in the Glistening Grotto

In a cave adorned with shimmer and sheen,
Echoes of laughter are often seen.
Stalactites drip, creating a beat,
While shadows parry in a comical feat.

Crickets play tunes on the damp rocky wall,
As droplets cascade with a joyful sprawl.
Laughter mingles with the sound of the stream,
In the glimmering depths, where giggles beam.

Bats swoop in with a playful flurry,
While echoes ring out in a jolly hurry.
With each flap and flutter, a cackle takes flight,
In the depths of the grotto, oh, what a sight!

Glistening gems hold secrets untold,
While the echoes of joy in the cave unfold.
Nature's own jesters, they dance in the dark,
In a laughter-filled grotto, igniting a spark.

Radiant Revelations of the Earth

Beneath a sky of canvas blue,
The soil whispers secrets, too.
With every spade, a giggle rolls,
Each worm a joker, playing roles.

Sunshine tickles blades of grass,
As beetles dance in leafy mass.
The daisies wink, bright and free,
Nature's jest for all to see.

Frogs jump high, then land in mud,
Creating splashes, frothy flood.
A squirrel pauses, waits for cheers,
While bees hum sweet, defying fears.

In forests deep, the shadows play,
Woodland sprites frolic all day.
Mirth is found in every nook,
Where earth and laughter share a book.

Serendipity in the Shade

Under branches, wild and wide,
Little creatures take their ride.
A chipmunk plays, a tiny thief,
Stealing seeds with comic grief.

Sunlight filters, kaleidoscope,
As shadows dance, a funny trope.
A lazy cat sprawls, then leaps high,
Chasing dust motes in the sky.

A rustle near the ferns so green,
A fox peeks out, a prankster keen.
Every corner holds a laugh,
In the wild, there's no tough path.

With every breeze that twists and twirls,
The air is filled with quirky pearls.
Nature's playhouse, free and bold,
Silly moments, worth their gold.

The Bounce of Blissful Breezes

Up above, the kites take flight,
In the wind, they dance with delight.
Children giggle, chasing tails,
As laughter rides on playful gales.

The sunbeams play peekaboo bright,
Turning shadows into light.
Leaves engage in a spirited chase,
A merry romp, a joyous race.

Butterflies weave through the air,
Their patterned wings, beyond compare.
Dragonflies prance, with flair and grace,
Joining in the day's embrace.

Each gust of wind a dear friend's call,
With giggles rising, towering tall.
In nature's arms, pure joy reveals,
The bounce of bliss, of spinning wheels.

Gusts of Mischief in the Green

In the coolness of the grove,
Whispers travel, secrets rove.
A squirrel teases, leaps with grace,
Challenging the wise old vase.

Twigs snap underfoot with cheer,
Every sound feels light and clear.
The bushes chuckle, leaves all sway,
As shadows lurk, ready to play.

A crow caws loud, a playful song,
Joining in, where all belong.
Grasshoppers giggle, leap and dart,
Nature's jesters, full of heart.

In every note, the earth's refrain,
It's all a joke, with no disdain.
Wrapped in greens, such tender schemes,
The world awakes, alive with dreams.

Merry Melodies of the Moss

In the woods where whispers play,
Beneath the ferns, we sway and sway.
A tickle from a secret breeze,
Makes fungi giggle as they tease.

The mushrooms dance on tiny feet,
While crickets chirp a merry beat.
Squirrels spin with joyful flair,
As laughter bounces in the air.

A robin cracks a silly joke,
While branches sway and trees provoke.
With every step, the ground will hum,
Nature's tune, we all become.

So let the mossy floor rejoice,
In nature's choir, we find our voice.
With every chuckle, every cheer,
Together here, we hold so dear.

Chirps of Joy in the Trees

High in the branches, antics unfold,
Chirpy tales and laughter told.
The leaves sway, a playful song,
Where every critter feels they belong.

A woodpecker dons a tiny hat,
While owls wink, and squirrels chat.
The sunbeams dance through all the green,
In every corner, giggles are seen.

Bouncy rabbits hop and skip,
While jays perform a clumsy flip.
With nature's jesters taking stage,
Joy erupts at every page.

So come, behold this leafy space,
Where every smile finds its place.
In soaring trees, heartbeats blend,
With laughter shared, there is no end.

Joy in the Hidden Corners

In shaded glens where secrets hide,
A funny face comes out to glide.
With every rustle, spirits sing,
From tiny bugs to bumblebees' wing.

A sunbeam slips through branches low,
Tickling toads who start to glow.
In every nook, a giggle's spun,
With all the mischief, oh what fun!

A shy old snail retracts with flair,
While butterflies tease without a care.
They flutter close, then zoom away,
Chasing joy throughout the day.

So find the corners, peek inside,
Where laughter plays, and dreams reside.
From tiny crickets to bold parade,
Nature's jesters have it made.

The Uplift of Nature's Heart

Nature's pulse, a vibrant beat,
With blooms and buzzes, oh so sweet.
The breeze, it tickles all around,
Where giggles echo from the ground.

The daisies wink with petals bright,
While clouds play tag with pure delight.
Sunflowers sway, a silly sight,
As shadows dance in morning light.

A jumping frog leaps with a splash,
While bees perform their buzzing bash.
In every flit and flutter near,
The heart of nature holds us dear.

So join the chorus, loud and free,
In nature's laughter, we all agree.
With every leaf that sways about,
The uplift joy brings is clear, no doubt.

The Play of Nature's Palette

In fields where colors blend and sway,
A splash of yellow brightens the gray.
The clouds above tease with shapes so grand,
As whispers of joy sweep across the land.

Tiny critters scurry and race,
Each one wearing a silly face.
Fluttering leaves join in the fun,
As sunbeams twinkle, laughter's begun.

Mushrooms appear with hats on their heads,
While rabbits hop where the dandelion spreads.
Nature chuckles, a symphony sweet,
In this place where the wild things meet.

Amidst the blooms, the bees take a spin,
Buzzing melodies, a lively din.
Each petal and stem plays its own part,
In the joyful canvas of nature's heart.

Giggling Glades of the Wild

In the glen where the wildflowers grow,
A breeze carries secrets, high and low.
The trees giggle softly, a rustling tease,
As shadows dance playfully upon the leaves.

A squirrel leaps, with acorn in tow,
Wobbly and wild in its frantic show.
Nearby, a brook chuckles, burbling clear,
While frogs in the reeds croak raucous cheer.

Bumblebees whirl in a dizzy parade,
Snapping their tiny legs, a grand charade.
Even the sunlight joins in the spree,
Painting the world in laughter's decree.

So take a stroll through these giggling glades,
Where humor and nature create escapades.
Embrace the whimsy that life has to bring,
In the heart of the wild, let joy take wing.

Nature's Unseen Chuckles

Beneath the fern, where shadows reside,
Nature's giggles in whispers abide.
A dappled light dances, winks with glee,
As petals unfold with playful esprit.

Each bee buzzing by delivers a jest,
While butterflies flit, all dressed in their best.
The droplets of dew sparkle, a playful gleam,
As if they're in on a delicate dream.

The rabbit who trips on soft blades of grass,
Turns to the skies, a comic alas!
A fox peeks around with a mischievous grin,
In this realm of laughter, the fun never thins.

So pause and listen, you might just hear,
The soft chuckles of nature, drawing near.
In each breeze and rustle, a joyful cheer,
In the world's endless comedy, find your sphere.

Daisies Dancing with Delight

In fields of white, the daisies sway,
With laughter woven in their ballet.
They nod and weave to the tune of the breeze,
While sunlit rays play hide and tease.

A ladybug twirls on a petal so fine,
Her spots like confetti, a merry design.
Honeybees hum a triumphant song,
As flowers rejoice in a raucous throng.

The butterflies join, their colors ablaze,
As the wind tells tales in whimsical ways.
With each gentle rustle, a chuckle can bloom,
In this garden of giggles where laughter finds room.

So dance with the daisies, let joy take flight,
In a world where each moment feels utterly bright.
Nature invites us to share in her cheer,
In this party of life, let's hold it all dear.

Smiles in the Shade

Beneath the branches, shadows play,
Silly whispers dance and sway.
A squirrel wears a nutty crown,
As giggles swirl and tumble down.

The sunlight beams with joy so bright,
While butterflies take graceful flight.
A snail slips past, all dressed in glee,
Wobbling 'round like he's fancy-free.

Jests in the Greenery

Among the ferns, a joke is told,
A breeze comes in, so soft, so bold.
The frogs all croak a funny tune,
While daisies clap beneath the moon.

A rabbit hops with such a flair,
Chasing shadows, light as air.
The flowers giggle in the breeze,
As nature's jesters dance with ease.

Mirth Moss-Draped

Mossy carpets hide and seek,
With tickles soft upon your cheek.
A hedgehog rolls with bristled cheer,
Wobbling 'round without a fear.

Laughter echoes through the trees,
As critters play and tease the bees.
A tumble here, a leap over there,
Joy is found everywhere!

Giggles of the Undergrowth

Beneath the leaves, the laughter sings,
As tiny creatures flit on wings.
A thousand stories shared in jest,
In patches wild, they're all the best.

The shadows chuckle, bright and spry,
As little ants scurry by.
A hedgehog winks with a knowing grin,
In this playful world, where joy begins.

Whimsical Wonders of the Wood

In the shade of trees so tall,
Squirrels plot their playful brawl.
Frogs in bow ties sing a tune,
While owls dance beneath the moon.

Mushrooms giggle, side by side,
Wobbling like they have a ride.
Birds in hats steal all the bread,
While beetles plan to dance instead.

Pinecones fall like tiny bombs,
And chipmunks flaunt their cheeky charms.
The forest seems to hum and sway,
In this jolly, wild ballet.

Underneath the leafy arch,
Nature hosts a laughing march.
With every rustle, smile and cheer,
Life here is a comedy dear.

Radiance in the Resting Green

Sunlight tickles blades of grass,
The ants parade as moments pass.
Worms wear hats made out of moss,
Swapping tales like they're the boss.

A butterfly's a clumsy kite,
Flipping, flapping, oh what a sight!
Dandelions bloom, a yellow cheer,
The chubby hedgehogs roll and steer.

A buzzing bee with a bright grin,
Sips sweet nectar, where to begin?
With laughter echoing so bright,
The garden's joy is pure delight.

Even shadows join the fun,
Creating shapes, oh what a run!
In every nook, joy can be found,
Where sparkling spirits dance around.

Ecstasy Among the Embracing Earth

Earthworms wiggle, singing low,
As tiny pixies put on a show.
Grass blades tickle toes and feet,
In this grassy field of sweet.

A daisy winks with petals bright,
While roly-polies roll with might.
Raccoons juggle shiny stones,
And giggles echo through the tones.

Clouds above wear fluffy hats,
While veiled in mist, the hare does prance.
A merry band, so lewd and spry,
Invites the moon to dance on high.

The roots below create a drum,
As moles emerge to join the fun.
Nature crafts a jolly scene,
In every crevice, joy is seen.

Romeo and the Woodland Faeries

In the glen, where fairies twirl,
Romeo leads with a gentle whirl.
A fawn with flowers on its head,
Dances where the sunlight spread.

Giggling sprites with wings so bright,
Play hide and seek till morning light.
They steal his shoes just for a lark,
And scatter sparkles in the dark.

The owls hoot in a funny way,
As he trips on roots in dismay.
With laughter bubbling through the trees,
Nature's joy is sure to please.

A night of fun, no need for sleep,
In this woodland, secrets keep.
Together they weave a tale so grand,
Of wonder woven through the land.

www.ingramcontent.com/pod-product-compliance
Lightning Source LLC
Chambersburg PA
CBHW051649160426
43209CB00004B/848